AF485173

The Little Leaves
of Autumn Blew

The Little Leaves
of Autumn Blew

Benjamin David Kuntzsch

First edition, 2026

ISBN: 979-8-9955867-0-8

www.benjamindavidkuntzsch.com

Here compiled
are the varied wanderings of my life,
representing the maturation
to which I am hitherto privy.

What a circuitous journey
in which I've gleaned,
along the path,
a sense of self.

May you read this work
at your heart's behest,
observing such benefits as you may.

Table of Contents

Alienation

I am weird and you are not
Is always what my mind has thought
Not a one can understand
The way in which I think I am

All alone on islands bare
Others cannot come and stare
You don't know me, if you did
You'd see I'm not a normal kid

So on this bluff of trees and sand
I will not budge, I will not stand
To get inside a skiff that's bent
Doubt abides and sureness rent

Someday soon I'll take a gander
Round the bend, a short meander
Maybe I'll just stay inside
My riddled heart becomes my pride

Though this sucks, I know it's true
I can't reveal myself to you
What would happen if you said
You're a stupid dumb dumb head!

Then I'd have to reinvent
My fallen world, I won't consent
Remain I will inside my head
Believing that I shan't be read

I fear to speak of hidden heart
Perhaps this here will be a start
To catalog my fears and jeers
Long enough that I can steer

Betrayal

Who am I
I do not know
All I do is quid pro quo

Independence lacking sure
I find myself enacting words
Of self-doubt grief and shame inside
My tenderness just cannot thrive

Deep down I am young at heart
In spirit I'm a burnt-up tart
My wizened riddled addled might
Has rendered me without a fight

Who am I
But what you say
Without your love I'm cast away

I alone don't hold the flag
Except of white when I am sad

So who am I
I ask again
A friend without a friend

Reconciliation

The devil isn't real I think
Except in me where I do shrink
At thoughts of what I might become
Without the people whom I love

If they approve, then I feel gay
If they reprove, then I will splay
My timid limbs upon the ground
Thence losing strength to dream without

If they do say that I am great
I will decide I can't berate
Unless perhaps I catch a whiff
Of someone who can see my rift

If someone spied my inner pride
I'd lose all sense of hope and drive
There'd be no way to loosen up
For tenderness would be amuck

Even still I've got the wall
Around it none can see at all
Thus lies uphold the confidence
Which circumvents my common sense

It seems I'll die a broken man
Unless perhaps I rend the rand
Which strengthens not my saddened stride
But strips me of my inner pride

Remove the shoes of hellish make
And break the shackles of self-hate
Refine in me a bitterness
Toward missives making me amiss!

The Inside Man

My mind contains an evil man
Who's searched his heart and called it sand
Yet in this man, there is a hope
That someday he will cease his mope

But always wins this tricksy worm
He teaches me I'll never learn
He tells me that I do not know
A single thing about my woe

He poisons me with doubt and grief
My sadness is a tank of reef
I see a shape of species grand
An urchin perchin' in a catamaran

Basking about, this Satan sleuth
Could lose if but he stayed aloof
However he is vigilant
Making me ambivalent

Abyss of despair stands right below me
The kraken is smacking his lips so morosely
Ending my hope is ever his wont
Leading me cross a plank of daunt

Sharply snap the jaws awaitin'
Serpentine surrender state 'tis
Don't you squirm you witless dolt
Didn't I tell ya, don't revolt!

Chronic

I'm in pain
I'm in pain
Every single fucking day

I will maim
I will maim
Revolutionarily

I'm in pain
I'm in pain
God damn it, I feel great!

I'll explain
I'll explain
How every seismic shift berates

I'm in pain
I'm in pain
Give me peace, O sullen frame

Longing

Without a doubt, I will amount
To more than scrap and metal
Fueled furnace that is learnèd
Thoroughly in *hevel*

I hope that I can make a change
If perhaps with rhyming
Music could direct my path
And give me fill and thriving

Without a doubt, I will evict
Viscount that sits inside redoubt
I'll liberate my saddened state
To cure my hellish gout!

But when will I become
More than a mere morsel miming.

Self-harm

I am the thorn
I'm filled with scorn
And longing more
Than ever for
Libertador
Who once before
Had strengthened sure
My wistful core

My fear of shore
Beyond the moor
Is filled with gore
And weight of yore
O what a bore
Trépidator

But who will moor
My ship to port
Resolve my lore
O Redentor

Stuck

I cannot focus nor abide
And so attempt to pen my pride
Is it pride or simply strife?
Am I estranged by feelings rife?

When will all this be constructed?
Maybe not till I've erupted
Will this ink ignite my flame?
At last to stand with solid frame?

I'm terrified my countenance
Will make me friendless scoundrel hence
Whither dost thine heart reside?
Over my feelings I ought to preside

Certainly, with certainty
I'll rend the fear that burdens me
I don't know why I'm so waylaid
Oppressive thoughts can't be parlayed

Spider

A web of tender protection
Wraps ever around my waist
It gives me not direction
But says I should make haste

Anxiety abounding
I think I found the bane
Funny and astounding
It's me that was the knave

Unscrupulous with hubris
I find my dreams curtailed
I don't think I can do this
A ship without a sail

Bescribbler

They call me the belittler
For I make myself a little hurt
With hardy taunts and heartfelt gaunt
I render mended fount enfaunt

They call me the beriddler
For I spin a web of lies
To grant myself a phantom skirt
Between yourself and I

They call me the bewhittler
For I make myself feel small
Dispelling all my love and mirth
No feelings come at all

Assurance

Certainly, with certainty
I'll rend the fear that burdens me
I don't know why I'm so waylaid
At times my fear is in the way

I lose a sense of inner drive
I get distracted and contrive
A dream which I cannot achieve
I don't know why I can't reprieve

A nail upon my mindstone forced
My feelings are a code of morse
What shall be when I have lost
Awareness that I am embossed

Maybe I will find the means
To compliment consistent preen
A little hope will give me spring
Perhaps someday I'll learn to sing

Wintering

Fallen trees in snow-filled fields
Paths of green remembered

Strengthened by bitter cold
Waiting for daybreak

Yet do not wait
Embrace that icy chill
Which sends a shiver down the spine

Learn
Grow
Do not cease
Do not be embittered to it

Leave the leaves alone for now
Let snow abound
And assert your wonder

Endeavor to become bold
In the wake of color
and warmth

Who am I?

I am the question
and the answer.

I am the fire
and the flood.

I am the unknown
and the known.

I am the thoughts
and the feelings.

I am the conch
and the crab
and the sea.

I am my name
and yet never will be.

I am my face
and yet truly am something more.

The Great Meander

Long roads
Ever winding
Predetermined paths

Will it be the road or the lands unseen?

Paths unchartered
Treacherous
Lonely

Did I choose the wrong way?
I should turn back

Up hills
Encountering all that I fear

Find the path
This was a mistake

I see others
I hear others
Even right next to me

But they walk their own path
Alone

What shall I do but press on?

I want to quit
It's too hard
But there's too much at stake

The woods become thickets of thorns
I get stuck for a while
Lost

Seasons change
The trees were bare

I see a light through trunks
Rising sun
A horizon

Thorns in my side
Striding through brambles

Up a hill
O'er the ramparts of despair

A luscious green valley awakens
Spring and rivers swim along
Birds are singing happy songs

Atop the tallest hill of grass, I cry
Grateful at the finding
The wandering

Biosphere

So, I come to the end of the beginning,
standing at the verge.

I find, as I walk into the Valley of Jubilation,
that some demons follow,
though they dare not linger too long
outside that obscureness of shame.

The final spritely runts pursue me,
but their qualms are more that of a familiar child
than the adult tail-chaser.

I address, with kindness and clarity,
the last vestiges of self-forsake,
recognizing that I have made every effort
in self-pursuit.

I cast aside my traveling cloak
and roll about in the grass,
singing in the meadows
and cartwheeling in a dale of twayblade.

I find rest on cold stone
in the fading warmth of a westward eye.

Stoking

The slate roof of a stone cottage
glimmers in the rising sun.

A lark sings atop a smokeless chimney,
warbling restive refrains.

A rickety door swings to and fro, unlatched,
while the pale shine alights a threshold.

I fall to my knees in an unkempt garden.
The fallow smells afresh,
whispering promises to my callused palms.

Long have I walked a trail
of intermittent madness,
feeling astray,
yet retaining some smallest ember.

The ember cooled.
And every time I inspected my clenched fist
in those dark woods,
I felt foolish for my hope.

Now, having returned from the brink,
I rekindle the flame.

Fear of Fear

Fear came knocking at the door
in an emerald cloak,
disguised as a messenger.

He asked to be invited in
but would not show his face before entering.

An old man,
tending to his lonely hearth,
unshackled the port of his stormy sea-boat
and bade the creature in.

It sat on the couch and waited.
The man stepped into the firelight
and took his chair.

The creature stared,
and slowly,
raising its hood,
showed the man a terrible sight.

The face was every horror he'd ever dreamed,
recurring and prognosticating new failures,
fornicating future furnishings and trinkets
for the triumphant Castle of Self-Domination.

This black hole of death
started a whirlwind of panic,
and the old man,
feeling faint,
began to fade.

At the final hour of his submission,
he found the strength to say:
Wait!
What are you?

At once, he saw himself staring back
with all the cuts and bruises
he'd ever borne.

He felt compassion,
and the creature,
fading to his younger self,
began to cry.

Forgotten Dreams Reprieved

I have journeyed to the center of my soul
and beseeched my inner woe.

I have pushed the boundaries of self-discovery
to the breaking point.

I cannot hide.
For as my self-doubt wanes,
a growing doubt of that doubt emerges.

I am prepared for the plunge,
concluding that it has just surpassed me.

Finding renewed freedom
from the burden of blame,
I charter a course toward self-love.

What a stupendous day!
Of recent, I recall the sentiments of Easter morn,
when people gather and bask in the thanksgiving
of rebirth and revelation.

Today is that day.
The journey through internal winters
becomes a journey without,
a journey imbued with pride
that restricts rumination,
establishing internal vigilance
that I might redact self-harm.

A Feast

I heard in the valley
A bell that could rally
The soul from afar
A feast! Bonsoir!

Sons came a-striding
Galloping, gliding
None were refused
Still some perused

The table was seated
But courage who'd bleated
Still striving atop the heather-moor

And one more person
For behind a curtain
Hurt was lurkin'

The party cried
Alive with pride:
Come out! Come out!
To this joyous feast
Mirth to all and you not least!

Losing all his bitter schemes
He whooped and realized:
It's the dream!
My longing and my great obsession
Joy and song have taught a lesson!

From the woods I came to spy
But overcome by tidings nigh
My cloak is hung up on the post
Let's dig in now to every roast!

Sweet delights
Of every type
Were passed to all
Throughout the night

Torches alighted
All had been righted
These merry times
Were very fine

Much to share post-reparations
Each had sought a destination
Now to find arrival sweet
Hurt did ask:
O would you please
Massage my back
And pass the cheese?

Freedom tap danced on the table
Knowing he was always able
Tension and Extension
Were the twins of great esteem
The bard behaved blithely
And kept them all lively

The twins were pantomime
The sublime dine
On vintage wine
Aligned the host to thankfulness

But most of all the painfulness
Of journey long
Was pardoned by
The lively throng

The prince at the head
Had smiled and said:
Come sit in my stead
I'll bake some more bread!

Hurt took the seat
began to eat
and contemplated every feat

A crown appeared atop his brow
He couldn't give a reason how
He smiled so delightedly
And looked around excitedly

All stared back with due esteem
The king had come to live his dream
The rightful heir to throne imagined
Thoughtful of the chair he sat in

The youngest king
The din did ding
A bell inside his strengthened mind:
Are really all these people mine?

The sound of footsteps near at hand
Anxiety came striding through
He passed the band
And knelt to who?

The child beguiled
Had rested awhile
His crown so soft
His dreams aloft

Courage stood there to the side
Prepared to scare if *he* should chide:
You got this!
Just wait and breathe
Remember you're the one who deems

Up he sat, the king descried
He felt his sturdy girded side
He realized that the messenger
No longer a confectioner
Protected now-unsullied harts
But still he gave a little start

Stand and tell me guardian
Whence come you so far again
Let the choir not be singing
O'er the statements you are bringing

The silent crowd now bent an ear
Listening replaced a leer

A bring a report instead of retort
I'm sorry I've spoken poor notions in past
But here I am, I've come at last

I'm here to offer services
A churlish self now cherishes
A circus not disparaging
Encourages such merrying

Bless me with this entourage
Bless me with a bon voyage!
Hear me free of consternation
Grateful for amalgamation

All were crying and laughing
The tumult amassing
These foals were surpassing
The holdings and mapping
The moldings of an edifice:
A place in which
To fly and wish
To wonder in safety
But never sedately

Still we'll have a pic-i-nic
And wander in the thick of it
Gallivanting out the door
Adventuring the forest floor!

Rabble rousing and rumpus
A chorus of trumpets ruckus
Was upsetting the muffin chef
So I stamped my feet
and said: *look left!*

I quick wrote a story
To calm all the quarries
I read it aloud
Astounding the crowd

Some parts gave laughter
Others were chapters
Of life in a dream unsown

From tantalized
To shutter-eyed
At rest the seven and ten
Dozed and dreamed a wren

The fire blazed
The stars gazed
Intrigued by the motley crew

The embers sang
The silence rang
The little leaves of autumn blew